INTRODUCTION

Since the dawn of time, mankind has been waging wars. From clashes between rival clans to the two great world conflicts – not forgetting the wars that punctuate the news – who is capable of establishing an exhaustive list? Enemies of a day become allies, allies become enemies, but with a regularity of a metronome, wars follow one another.

Another constancy, since mankind has domesticated them he has invited the horse, his noblest conquest, to participate. The cavalry was quickly revealed as the centerpiece of any dignified army worthy of its name. Warriors "on horseback", secular masters of the battlefields, were thus appointed Knights in the Middle Ages. Crowned for his success, the horse enjoys a place of first choice in military tradition and numerous kings and warlords were represented for posterity on their proud mount. The Republican guard, the iconic unit, proves how, even today, the horse remains prestigious.

Others joined them. Simple pack animals, animal-tools or "weapons" of war, have demonstrated amazing abilities of adaptation and have, over time, filled a great diversity of missions alongside the fighters.

During the mobilisation of the summer 1914, the animal soldiers should have been entitled to claim a well-deserved rest: more enduring motorised vehicles, more powerful, more deadly and important progress in the means of communication seemed likely to spare them a new campaign. It was not to be, and more than 14 million animals, of which more than 10 million equidae were mobilised during the Great War even if these figures, due to a lack of reliable censuses, remain an estimate to be considered with caution. These vehicles, however modern, could not substitute the animals for certain missions or on certain military operations. These Revolutionary means of communication showed their limits on the upturned battlefields. So there was no substitution but rather a form of complementarity: what some were unable to accomplish was entrusted to others.

Many fighters bequeathed to us their testimonials. They help us today to understand – or at least to try to understand – what men endured in 1914-18, but no animal could testify of his own experience, nor share with us his emotions. Only archival photographs, objects and the gaze of the soldiers they rubbed shoulders with allow us to see what was the Great Animal War.

✦ Bronze statue of Jeanne d'Arc.
Historial de la Grande Guerre, Péronne.

THE MISSIONS

THE CAVALRY

In August 1914, the high command planned a short war of movement in which the cavalry, whose speed and impact had proved themselves over the centuries, will hold an essential role. The question remained, did they have the numbers necessary, The maintenance of a cavalry proved costly in times of peace and the army can not count on it's herd alone. It must therefore, through mobilisation, complement its workforce. Many horses were requisitioned (700,000 from August to December 1914, or 20% of the French horses available). These requisitions necessary for the proper conduct of the war, however, are not without consequence in the countryside. In a society largely rural, the horse – and often the only horse in small farms – is an indispensable tool for the work on the farms. Already deprived of the men, his departure leaves the family helpless. It was with regret that they entrusted their horse to the army and the recommendations that the owners gave (how to feed him, caress him) at the moment of separation illustrated the special status of the horse at the time. Pauline Lombard, then a child, remembers eighty years later: "My grandfather had a horse, Kid, a handsome brown horse with a long tail, and an uncle a horse named Bijou. I loved them a lot and cried when they were gone. My grandfather wanted to console me: Do not cry, they will come back soon. We did not seen them again"(Family archives).

But some of the freshly enlisted horses did not have the predispositions required for the tough military life imposed on them. Many were unfit and, after two months of campaign, the cavalry deplored the loss of many animals even when engagements on the battlefield had been rare. Draft horses accustomed to intense efforts on a limited time or thoroughbreds able to hold a fast pace over short distances struggled to accomplish the long marches imposed on them: some units traveled up to one hundred and eighty kilometers in three days. Rarely unsaddled, insufficiently watered, the beasts tired and more than ten thousand died of exhaustion under the hot sun of the first summer of war – over the duration of the conflict, all causes combined, on average, three hundred horses died every day, almost five million in total.

✦ Order of requisition of horses and mules in the municipality of Doullens, Somme, 1914. The order specifies that the owners must bring their horses with bridle, halter provided with a lanyard and horseshoes in good condition. Historial de la Grande Guerre, Péronne.

✦ Postcard: "Keep my man at war as long as you wish, but at least leave me my mare !!!". "Historial de la Grande Guerre", Péronne. Behind its humorous tone, the postcard emphasises the status of farm horses and the unpopularity of military requisitions.

"He had no back [my] unhappy [horse], he was hurting so much, just two plates of flesh remained in place under the saddle, as wide as my hands and oozing, too bright with great trails of puss that flowed from under the blanket to its hocks. But we had to trot on, one, two... He squirmed with every movement" (*Journey to the end of the night* – Louis-Ferdinand Céline).

The war of movement for the first months offered the cavalry a preponderant role in reconnaissance operations. But on the field of battle, the cavalry fought unequally against machine guns and rapid fire artillery; accustomed to see his charge put the enemy in flight, his own ranks are now decimated before they can even get close. "The enemy attacked with the cavalry [...]. We saw the wave rise from the bowl, rise, a single roll of heavy scum! It moved slowly, contained in an inconceivable expectation, under the hail, the downpour and the storm of German infantry and batteries. [...] On two ranks, the riders, lances at the oblique, and then lowered for the shock. One animal falls, another crowns itself, another overturns, a rider falls to the ground, another is dragged along the ground, his boot in the stirrup. A breach broke out, four horses are struck on the first row. And six, eight, nine are swept on the flank, a pile of convulsing kicks. [...] And then the fires in all this heap [...] That's where the parade ends." (*L'ordre du jour* – Edlef Köppen).

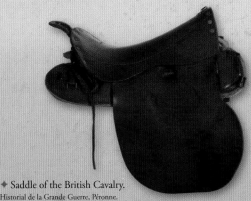

✦ Saddle of the British Cavalry.
Historial de la Grande Guerre, Péronne.

✦ French Cavalry patrol, end of 1914.
Historial de la Grande Guerre, Péronne.

✦ Uniform of a French Cavalry, 1914.
Historial de la Grande Guerre, Péronne.

✦ The Imperial Camel Corps leaving Egypt, 1917. Australian War Memorial, Canberra.

Unable to impose their force on the battlefield and facing the growing need in the infantry and artillery, the first cavalry squadrons are dismantled in autumn 1915: almost two thousand horsemen are transferred to the infantry and nearly four thousand to the artillery. This trend is confirmed and in July 1916 just 495 remained of the 718 Cavalry squadrons listed just ten months before. Many "dismounted" riders turned towards the aviation and, in a smaller proportion, towards the tanks, where they found in part in the aerial duel the chivalrous spirit that they had abandoned in the trenches. "But who were these aviators? They came from the gigantic army exposed in the Front Line trenches to incessant shelling and they constituted an elite gathered together by a need for ever bolder forms of combat. They were also riders, silhouettes emaciated from familiar equestrian competitions, with their chiseled faces and monocles sparkling. They were tired of rotting in the villages and castles at the rear and of waiting for the resumption of the march forward." (Ernst Jünger, *The Boqueteau 125*). Obvious similarities are found when comparing the position of the rider on his mount and that of the aviator in the cockpit of his aircraft.

Men have rode other mounts. Dromedaries for example, better adapted than horses to the vast expanses of sand of North Africa. Constituted in January 1916, the Imperial Camel Corps was composed of four Australian, British and New Zealand battalions having participated in the Gallipoli campaign in the Dardanelles in 1915. These camelids, estimated to over a thousand, performed at first reconnaissance patrols in Egypt and then participated in some skirmishes against local tribes before being engaged in 1917 in Sinai against the troops of the Ottoman Empire. The Imperial Camel Corps was partly dismantled in June 1918 to form two new Australian cavalry regiments on the Western Front.

THE HUSSARS OF DEATH

Favorite headdress of Crown Prince Wihlem, eldest son of the German Kaiser Wihelm II, the busby is made in part from expensive furs (otter, opossum...). traditional German hussars Cap, it participates in their prestige. Three of their elite regiments - Wilhelm II personally provides command of the 1st Regiment - proudly sports an impressive skull intended to impress the opponent, or better still to terrify him. While the Great War saw the metal helmet replace the old headdresses favouring aesthetics, the Hussars of Death keep their fetish busby.

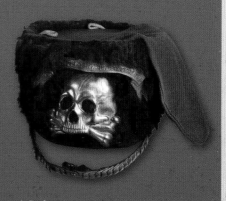

✦ Busby. Historial de la Grande Guerre, Péronne.

✦ A Decauville locomotive being replaced by horses to enter into the zone of fighting, Hesse Forest, 22 July 1915. BDIC, Fonds Valois.

THE DELIVERY OF MATERIAL

To be operational, an army must rely on strong stewardship to supply the front with soldiers, equipment, weapons, ammunition... from the rear to the military zone, motorised vehicles were used almost exclusively and to the full. Trains and trucks were able to quickly transport on long distances large amounts of soldiers and materials (the most striking example and the more emblematic remains undoubtedly that of the Sacred way during the Battle of Verdun where the convoy moved day and night without stopping). But the animals took over when approaching the Front Line where horses, mules and others became indispensable.

A battery of artillery, in perpetual movement, employed thousands of horses. When France entered the war, a third of the horses were already assigned to the artillery regiments. A battery - and one regiment had nine – included in theory one hundred and sixty-eight horses. It took no less than six to tow the one thousand five hundred kilos of the French 75cm gun (though four may

✦ Artillery of the 75 gains its position, 1915.
Historial de la Grande Guerre, Péronne.

be sufficient on a motorised terrain), and ten for a 155 mm gun. "The artillery were marching, shaken by the jolts. Unperturbable, Forcibly braked guns slid down the streets. The helmets and the bodies of the gunners trembled. Horses, in the wake of the batteries, buttressed their hooves against the pavement, resisting stride after stride the thrust of steel". (*Way of sacrifice* – Fritz von Unruh).

During the battles of Verdun and the Somme in 1916, the material takes a more and more prominent roll; the need of horses for the artillery continued to grow and they alone mobilised almost half of the equine population. Requisitions where therefore regularly carried out at the rear but, not to jeopardize the economic activity of the country, 30% of the horses were also bought from abroad (particularly in the United States and in Argentina) during the four years of war.

Other animals, sometimes less expected, also participated in the delivery of material according to their particular abilities to adapt to certain sectors of the front.

Donkeys and mules were frequently used on mountainous fronts where their ability to climb slopes, greater than that of horses, excelled. This was the case in Alsace, on the front of the Vosges and in the Italian Alps. according to estimates, nearly 300,000 donkeys and mules participated in the Great War but no statistics give a reliable record of losses.

In 1914, especially in the Belgian army, there were sections of dogs for machine guns. Less visible by their small size than horses and mules when approaching the trenches. However, Belgian mastiffs had the great disadvantage of barking in the teams, informing the German defenders of their presence. The latter, having estimated the position of the sections approaching, reduced them to silence with artillery fire. The experiment was a failure and was quickly abandoned.

✦ Jardin des Tuileries, Paris 1916, from the "Sociéties de Prépartion militarie", annual review.
Parisienne de photographies © Maurice-Louis Branger / Roger-Viollet.

✦ Military kennels. Historial de la Grande Guerre, Péronne.

✦ Below: Donkeys with food supplies near the Front Line, 1916.
Historial de la Grande Guerre, Péronne.

The harsh winter of 1914-1915 made it difficult to refuel the trenches on the Front Line of the Vosges and cut the soldiers from their bases in the rear. In August 1915, Captain Moufflet and Lieutenant Haas crossed the Atlantic and returned from Alaska with 436 sled dogs. Upon their landing in Le Havre in December 1915, the famous musher Scotty Allan, whose help was invaluable in choosing and repatriating dogs in France, formed and lead in just a few weeks sixty teams and their drivers. In the snow or on narrow railways when the terrain became feasible, the help of the "Alaskan Poilu" would be preponderant to hold, and sometimes to retake, the Vosges mountains.

Other animals, much more anecdotal, but even more surprisingly, can be evoked. Elephants for example. Taken from circuses or zoos, these pachyderms were employed for ploughing the fields to compensate the absence of horses or, closer to the front, to move heavy loads. It was on the German's side, perhaps more affected by the lack of horses following the British blockade prohibiting importation from abroad, that the use - marginal it must be repeated, of elephants were the most common.

✦ Dogs from Alaska harnessed to a sledge, Le Collet, 1916.
BDIC, Fonds Valois.

✦ "An elephant placed in the services of the Generalissimo and employed for transporting tree trunks on the French battlefields", *Illustrierter Kriegs Kurier*, No. 23, 1915.
Historial de la Grande Guerre, Péronne.

ASSISTING THE WOUNDED

Like horses, dogs were mobilised from the beginning of the conflict. Initially, they were responsible for finding the wounded abandoned on the battlefield. A few military dogs had already proven their know-how in fulfilling this mission during the Boer War or the Russo-Japanese War. In August 1914, the French army had just over two hundred dogs capable of finding, in large spaces and often at night, the wounded that the stretcher-bearers could not locate, New dogs were enlisted and the workforce goes up to more than six hundred in early 1915. The number of dogs enlisted to fulfill various missions during the Great War is estimated at that of twelve thousand. During their training, they were trained to recover a personal effect of the injured to then take it back to the stretcher bearers to signal their discovery. The last stage was, of course, to direct the rescuers to the wounded.

Obviously, as a good patriot, the dog was educated to differentiate injured friends and injured foe. He must ignore the second and leave them to their sad fate. The "every man for himself" was the rule!

When the war was bogged down in the trenches, the search for wounded was facilitated by the reduced area of no man's land where the dogs had become an easy target for the opposing lines. The use for the dogs was abandoned but remained present in assisting the wounded. Attached to an evacuation cart, they participated as the mules and the donkeys, but to a lesser extent, in the evacuation of the wounded.

✦ Decorative plate, the first aid dogs, illustrated by Benjamin Rabier* for the soldiers of the 6th Arrondissement. Historial de la Grande Guerre, Péronne.
*See also page 16.

✦ Lead figurines of mules with stretchers evacuating the wounded, CBC Mignot. Historial de la Grande Guerre, Péronne.

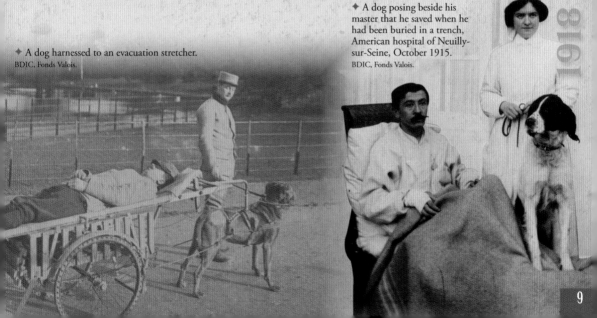

✦ A dog harnessed to an evacuation stretcher. BDIC, Fonds Valois.

✦ A dog posing beside his master that he saved when he had been buried in a trench, American hospital of Neuilly-sur-Seine, October 1915. BDIC, Fonds Valois.

1914 1915 1916 1917 1918

As soon as the front was immobilised, the missions of military dogs were adapted to the war of position. Their olfactory and especially auditory predispositions, far superior to those of man, were put to use. In a very loud environment, they were able to distinguish unusual noises or noises too weak for the human ear. Even before the danger could be perceived visually from the trench, dogs were able to hear or feel, and report the approach of an enemy patrol. On each side of no man's land, sentinel dogs assisted the watchmen to monitor the no man's land.

The task, carried out in a hostile and stressful environment, required a high degree of concentration. Rest periods were necessary to maintain their effectiveness especially with the continuous artillery shelling. As with fighters, their ears are under severe strain and dogs, in whom the gun-fire had disturbed the hearing, were found in the long run unfit to continue.

Many other animals proved effective in alerting soldiers of imminent danger. The undeveloped sense of smell warns them late, sometimes too late, of the arrival of poison gas; by detecting them much earlier, the animals provided valuable time for the soldiers to put on their protective masks: "Before being sent to France, the unit was garrisoned in the tropics and that's where they picked up Tommy, the mascot of the company. I dunno exactly what sort of animal it was but the closest would be a raccoon. According to Sergeant Halligan, in Honduras they called them the great anteaters. I could not say, but what I do know is that Tommy was more savvy than Captain Matlock and all his officers put together.

✦ French Grenadier and his sentinel dog, Front of Aisne.
Historial de la Grande Guerre, Péronne.

We were all sleeping in a shelter when a sentry sniffed the air, panicked and alerted gas. Everybody pulled on their masks and sat waiting until the tightness of the mask caused a migraine. I finished by realising that Tommy continued to sleep peacefully in a ball while the whole shelter was in a state of panic. He had no need to be warned by a sentinel: he just had to dig a hole in the ground and bury his muzzle. Once I understood that, I never paid any attention to the alerts that Tommy did not did confirm. And I never got gassed." (William March, Company K).

But the warning signs were not always understood by men: horses turning back in front of the threat of toxic clouds were whipped by their riders who attributed the behaviour of their mounts to a refusal of obedience.

✦ Sentinel dog at Neufvy-Sur-Aronde, 1915.
BDIC, Fonds Valois.

✦ British messenger dog bringing a message to his master after crossing the canal, Nieppe wood, 19 May 1918. BDIC, Fonds Valois.

Forerunners in the field, the Germans and Austrians already used messenger dogs in 1914. We had to waited until the summer of 1915 for such couriers to be used by the French and British. Each army had its own idea of educating the messenger dogs favouring either the autonomy of the dog or the link that united the man to the animal. The dogs showed great ability to adapt; where men struggled and took considerable risks to complete the delivery, dogs, smaller and lighter, sneaked with agility along the upturned ground and through the trenches in record time. Their success had its ups and downs because of the incessant movement of the troops which forces them when arriving in a new sector to build new landmarks; a period of acclimatisation was necessary before returning to work.

✦ Message coat for German messenger dogs. The message is placed under the upper part that opens and closes thanks to six press studs.
Historial de la Grande Guerre, Péronne.

The French army enlisted more and more messenger dogs. The numbers in their own kennels became insufficient, and it became necessary to take dogs from the pounds and shelters. These dogs, either once strays and often little inclined to obey the command of man, or breeds that were reluctant to this type of exercise, arrived directly on the front and to be trained "On the job". Not all meet the expectations. The army also called upon the dogs' masters and anxious to help with the war efforts over ten thousand dogs joined the front. "Newspapers have announced that Germans used war dogs, well-trained wolf-dogs, a blue-white red league at the rear appealed to the patriotic feelings well known to French women, and all those who had already given their son, their brother, their

CHIENS DE GUERRE

L'armée demande des chiens qui rendent de grands services. Faites des économies de nourriture et donnez vos chiens de berger et de garde âgés de un an à six ans. Évitez un déplacement inutile en n'offrant pas de chiens de chasse.

Pour tous renseignements, écrivez au Directeur du Chenil de Recrutement de Caen, à Bretteville-le-Rabet, par Langannerie (Calvados).

✦ Military appeal to civilian dog owners. It must be noted the economic argument used by the military to persuade dog owners who hesitated: Giving your dog, means no longer having to feed him!. Departmental Archives of Calvados, 20FI330.

fiance, their husband, their father or their lover, or their cousin, godson, nephew, had given in and sacrificed their dogs in the name of patriotism". (*La Main coupée* – Blaise Cendrars).

In addition to these dogs, the army relied on homing pigeons. One thousand five hundred pigeons provided, from the beginning of 1915 the transmission of messages in the rear. Their numbers grow rapidly and sixty thousand would

be mobilised for the French army during the conflict. About twenty thousand would loose their lives, victims of shrapnel, gas, enemy shooters, and sometimes birds of prey (predators naturally present in the area or raised by the enemy to eliminate them). They were progressively brought to the front line trenches due to their capacity to provide communication and deliver the messages when the phone lines were cut by shell explosions or when the use of optical telegraph was impossible due to thick smoke or fog.

The flight of the homing pigeon is not innate. It requires great apprenticeship and as with the dogs, each army had its own idea of their abilities. The British were convinced that pigeons could not make journeys at night and did not train them for this type of mission; the French, on the contrary, thanks to the strong homing pigeon tradition among the populations of North France and Belgium, achieved this with an interesting success rate. The extraordinary capacity of the homing pigeons to orientate allowed the pigeon to regularly change areas without harming their effectiveness.

Numerous mobile dovecotes, adapted Berliet double decker buses, crisscross the front and the pigeons showed how much their flight speed (average 60 km / h) and their constancy (few were lost) made valuable auxiliaries.

✦ Receptacle ring for messages.
Historial de la Grande Guerre, Péronne.

✦ Lead figurine of a Pigeon soldier and his dog carrying on its flanks two baskets to carry pigeons. CBC Mignot.
Historial de la Grande Guerre, Péronne.

A ZEALOUS PHOTOGRAPHER

In a war where everyone hides in trenches, it was nevertheless essential to be able to observe the opposing positions: numbers, movements and defenses need to be discovered. This was one of the first roles of the new born aviation. In equipping homing pigeons with an automatically triggered camera, it could be hoped, if luck was present – to obtain precious images. The results were revealed inconclusive on the battlefield and experience, initiated at the beginning of 20th century, remained marginal. Should we not see in this strange set-up the ancestor of our current drones?

✦ German homing pigeon equipped with a camera.
German Federal Archives, CC BY SA 3.0.

Efficiency, discretion, so many qualities required in a good spy. Concerned by the possibility of the civilian populations ability to communicate with allies through pigeons, the German authorities prohibited any possession or use. The poster here opposite, brought to the attention, and reminds of the interdiction to deter those who took the warning lightly, of the risks involved: fine, imprisonment and even death if there is evidence of espionage. Paul Busiere, for example, was shot on August 23, 1915 in Liévin for having a homing pigeon.

PROCLAMATION

Ces temps derniers on a trouvé a plusieurs reprises des pigeons, qui ont été jetés par des aviateurs francais ou au moyen de ballons sur le territoire occupé.

Ces pigeons et tous autres — non seulement pigeons-voyageurs — encore détenus illégalement, doivent être immédiatement livrés à l'Autorité Militaire Allemande la plus proche.

Sera puni:

1. — Celui qui trouve des pigeons ou leur équipement (panier, parachute, tube à dépêche, mode d'emploi, etc.) et qui ne les livre pas immédiatement à l'Autorité Militaire Allemande.

2. — Celui qui, ayant connaissance d'une telle trouvaille, ne l'annonce pas à l'Autorité Allemande.

3. — Celui qui fait envoyer des pigeons.

La tentative est punissable!

Toute contravention à ces prescriptions, **avec preuve d'espionnage**, sera punie de la peine de Mort ; **sans preuve d'espionnage**, sous les chiffres 1 à 3, par la réclusion ou l'emprisonnement d'au moins 2 ans; les cas de moindre importance seront punis d'au moins 3 mois de prison indépendamment d'une amende pouvant s'élever à 45.000 marks.

Les communes dans lesquelles se produiront les contraventions au présent ordre pourront aussi, comme punition, avoir à supporter des contraintes sensibles.

Fait au Quartier Général de l'Armée, le 25 Novembre 1917.

Pour le Général Commandant en Chef:

WICHURA,
General der Infanterie.

✦ Poster displayed in the headquarters of the German Army, in the occupied zone, 25 November 1917.
"Historial de La Grande Guerre", Péronne.

✦ Mobile dovecote Berliet, called Araba, 1915. The lower part of the vehicle allowed to accommodate the pigeon fancier and store the food of his protégés. Historial de La Grande Guerre, Péronne.

✦ Good friends. Historial de La Grande Guerre, Péronne.

✦ "An idyll in the forest, in Russia: a foal, a young fawn and a boars, nursed and fed by German soldiers", Illustrierter Kriegs Kurier, No. 15, 1916. Historial de La Grande Guerre, Peronne.

By donning the uniform, men are forced to break with the usual codes of peacetime. Away from home, emotional bonds were put to one side: a new life started. Subject to almost permanent stress, the soldiers found comfort with the animals, an outlet for the violence that allowed them to find the sweetness of life of yesteryear. Affection given, affection received, the links they wove with those companions of misery went beyond the simple military cadre. They were feed and cuddled. Animals of all kinds lived so close to the men in the trenches and in the cantonments: dogs and stray or abandoned cats, birds, tamed foxes…

"A small flat head slips under my arm. A white kitten, with a pink nose, purrs against my side. He stares at me with his beryl eyes, shows with a yawn the curve of his tongue, closes its eyes and goes to sleep. [...] I [...] caress the small ball of warm fur snuggled in my lap. The moment sends me into a daydream, and for an instant those daydreams seem real" (*Ceux de 14* – Maurice Genevoix).

"Baptiste is my raven, or rather the raven of the regiment. But it is obvious that I am his best friend. From the moment I appear, in the morning, he sees me. Despite my attempts, changing my times, finding different places to trick him, I am spotted. He hurriedly hops and beats his half-cut wing. He knows that I can not resist his mimicry, his half-open beak erect towards me, his head leaning to one side. Indeed, I will go to the kitchen for a piece of meat while he waits for me. As soon as I come out, he revolves around me making short leaps. He engulfs the piece with a short raspy groan expressing his pleasure. The swallowing done, he reopens his beak." (*La Sainte Face* – Elie Faure).

Remarkable testimonies show how much their presence was dear to men, how much they were attached to these companions in misfortune. An example was the Tommies that made it their duty to give a grave to the young piglet they had befriended, after it had been killed by shrapnel. So many men did not have this luck !
To hear the singing of birds, follow the flight of a butterfly or the antics of a squirrel in a tree, were simple pleasures that gave the troops a few moments of escape and dreaming.

✦ Varnished plaster statuette of a French hunter playing with a puppy, A. Corio. Historial de La Grande Guerre, Péronne.

✦ Arrival of cattle at the slaughterhouse, Fellering, 8 August 1916. BDIC, Fonds Valois.

THE NOURISHING HERD

Food was a daily concern for the fighters. Necessary for thier good health it was a spring of first importance for their morale. An article in the newspaper The Illustration in 1917, predicts that "victory will belong to that of the two belligerents who has in its reserve, a month or more of food than the other". Created on August 2, 1914, the automobile service of the French army devoted one of its sections – the RVF – to the supply of fresh meat: the soldier's daily rations included fresh or frozen meat and seasoned canned meat (the famous "singe" – monkey meat – to take up the slang of the French "Poilu"). Convoyed in wagons from the rear to the army slaughterhouses, oxen, sheep, pigs and others were slaughtered and cut into quarters before being delivered by RVF buses to the regimental canteens.

Although the stewardship of the canteen was in place, soldiers regularly complained of the quality of the food: "Ah! mates, the barbecue they gave us yesterday, talk about knives to a stone! Beef steak, that? Rubber soles more like. I said to the guys: *careful, you others ! Do not chew too fast; you'll break your teeth; sometimes the cobbler forgets to pull out all the nails! [...]* - From time to time, so that you cannot complain that it is hard, we were served something soft and sticky, like poultice; a sponge that had no taste. When you bite on it, it was like you were drinking water, nothing more nor less."(Henri Barbusse, *"le Feu"*, newspaper of a squadron).

✦ Loading quarters of beef in a RVF bus, Fellering, 8 August 1916. BDIC, Fonds Valois.

Men waited impatiently for the packages sent by their families, which they usually shared with their camrades, or they obtained supplies directly, even if they complain about abuses, from the civilians in villages where they were confined: "... they extorted huge amounts of money from us. You only had to see the amount of money going into the villages around Bethune which, for several months had already sheltered about one hundred thousand men. [...] Every ten days every soldier of class two, received a five franc note (almost four shillings) that he immediately spent on eggs, coffee and beer in the neighbouring villages. The prices were exorbitant and the drink awful." (*Good-bye to all that* – Robert Graves).

From time to time, hunting, fishing and poaching completed every day life: "Garnéro was a clever hunter and a fine cook. He could not see a cat without sending him a bullet in the neck and, after having exposed it to a night of frost, he prepared it

✦ A Fishing party of gunners from the 117th Regiment, 1915. This fishing party has been immortalised several times. In this last shot, the men stage themselves and take the pose. It's 1 April 1915! On the back of the photograph intended for his wife Jeanne, Henri Omas (squatting on the bank) writes in pencil: "The fish aren't biting much, but we have papers ones for the operator". Family archives.

for us. We ate two, three a week! All the cats that wandered in the abandoned ruins of the villages on the front, went in the saucepan of Garnéro, and we feasted". (*La main coupée* – Blaise Cendrars).

NOTHING TO MAKE A FUSS ABOUT

Benjamin Rabier, famous illustrator assigned to RVF, imagines a hilarious cow head (cow - Vache in French) in response to the contest launched to creat an emblem for the regiment. It is inspired by the emblem of the German transport troop: the Walkyries, iconic gods of mythology Germanic. Changing Walkyrie to Wachkyrie, there is only one step that Benjamin Rabier does not hastens across. His design, original and easy to identify, is also an opportunity to mock the enemy.

In 1921, Léon Bel, also mobilised in the RVF, creates a melted cheese, inspired by the emblem of the RVF to impersonate it and introduced the brand "*Vache qui Rit*" – The Laughing Cow. In 1923, he asked Benjamin Rabier to redo the logo, he added the earrings and bought the copyrights for one thousand francs. But the big smile of the animal remains enigmatic: is she happy to take the bus for the first time, or is she a snub addressed to the Germans? The mystery remains...

✦ Partition cover of a song by Pierre d'Armor, "The Wachkyrie", illustrated by Benjamin Rabier, 1919. On the left of the page it says: "Remembrance of war, insignia of the R.V.F. / B.70, supply truck for fresh meat". Historial de la Grande Guerre, Péronne.

✦ Soldiers of the B70 section of the RVF, posing in front of their supply truck.

THE SUFFERINGS

"DESPITE OURSELVES"

✦ Otto Dix, *Horse carcass etching*, Der Krieg, 1924.
Historial de la Grande Guerre, Péronne © ADAGP, Paris 2018.

When leaving their homes, men knew they were leaving for war, why they were going to do it and welcomed it willy-nilly. Even if few of them at the moment of their departure are prepared for what awaits them, they were aware of risks they incurred. Animals, on the other hand, were immersed into a hostile environment that was unknown to them and that they could not understand. Unlike men, they had no cause to defend, no objective that could justify such a cataclysm. The enrollment of these "despite ourselves" affected the men: "The spectacle of mules and dead horses upset me: human corpses, all that was well and good, but it seemed to me ignoble to lead in that way animals into the war. (Robert Graves, *Goodbye to all that*).

If the suffering of the comrades was accepted with resignation, that of the animals inspired pity, compassion, and sometimes even indignation: "A shell somewhere fell into the dugout. Cries are heard between successive blows. [...] These were not human beings who could scream so

✦ German horses and riders equipped with gas masks, *Das Leben Im Bild*, No. 27, 1918.
Historial de la Grande Guerre, Péronne.

terribly. Kat says: Injured horses. I have never heard horses crying and I could hardly believe it. It's all the distress of the world. It's the martyred creature, it's a wild and terrible pain that moans like that. We had become pale. Deterring stood up: In the name of God! Finish them then! He was a farmer and he knew horses. It affected him dearly. And, as if on purpose, the bombing became almost silent and the animals cries more and more distinct." (*All quiet on the Western Front* – Erich Maria Remarque).

The animals shared with the fighters the fear, the same sufferings and for many therefore, the same tragic destiny. The losses are difficult to establish precisely but if you refers to the single mortality rate of horses, and if this rate was proportionally similar to that of the combatants, the French army would not have deplored 1.3 million deaths but near 4 million !

The first associations for the protection of animals appeared in France in the middle of the XIXth century. But it was the British public opinion who was the first to be indignant against the treatment and the fate reserved for horses of war. Some newspapers denounce the "Waste of requisitioned horses" and it was the initiative of British companies that the first veterinary positions were installed near the front in the fall of 1914.

✦ Horse burial, country side 1914.
Historial de la Grande Guerre, Péronne.

✦ Bloodletting of a horse being treated in a German veterinary station, *Illustrierter Kriegs Kurier*, No. 31, 1916.
Historial de la Grande Guerre, Péronne.

✦ Examination of a wounded dog in a British veterinary station. Historial de la Grande Guerre, Péronne.

BLUE CROSS FUND
HELP THE WOUNDED HORSES AT THE WAR

"OUR DUMB FRIENDS' LEAGUE"
A SOCIETY FOR THE ENCOURAGEMENT OF KINDNESS TO ANIMALS
DONATIONS IMMEDIATELY TO
ARTHUR J. COKE, Secretary.
58, VICTORIA STREET, LONDON, S.W.

OUR FRIENDS THE ANIMALS

In Great Britain, the Blue Cross was committed to raising funds to endow veterinary services with personnel, equipment, medication... It thus compensated for the inadequacies of the armed forces in the care of the suffering or injured animals. The French Ministry of War, aware of its shortcomings, supported the beneficent action of these companies and recommended doing everything possible to facilitate their actions.

✦ Blue Cross Fund. "help the wounded horses at the war".
Historial de la Grande Guerre, Péronne.

✦ Bed with a mesh flap designed by a soldier for protection against the rats during his sleep, *The Miroir*, No. 171, 4 March 1917.
Historial de la Grande Guerre, Péronne.

THE PROFITEERS OF WAR

"France had three enemies: the Boche, the rats and the flies", said a deputy during a meeting sitting in parliament. Perhaps he could have added a fourth: the louse. To the violence of battlefield, deplorable conditions there were indeed factors of additional discomfort and stress. If the man to man fighting seemed fair, that against the pests was a lost cause: "Here, in front of me, is a week where my role of combat will be circumscribed in the fight against flies and rats. I will be defeated in this unequal fight, as a result of considerable amount of reinforcements sent every minute by the enemy, on the battlefields." (Henri Barbusse, in a letter to his wife 1914-1917).

True "war profiteers", these enemies, as Henri Barbusse called them, evolved in an environment conducive to their proliferation and no fighter's testimony failed to evoke them. All report, noting their helplessness to stem the phenomenon, the long sessions stripping, laundry or the passage of clothing into the flames.

A HISTORY OF "TOTO"

The insecticide powder Zara had the merit of being harmless to man. Its efficiency was however relative against lice. If it repulses the unwanted guests, it did not attack the eggs and revealed itself as ineffective.

✦ Box of insecticide powder "l'Obus", registered trademark. Length: 8 cm.
Historial de la Grande Guerre, Péronne.

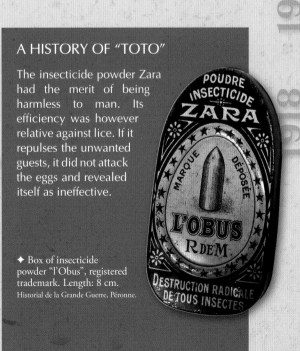

POUDRE INSECTICIDE ZARA
MARQUE DÉPOSÉE
L'OBUS R DE M
DESTRUCTION RADICALE DE TOUS INSECTES

If lice and rats are incessant torments, the latter, beyond the inconvenience they cause, inspired real disgust: "... a huge rat scooted or rather brushed his head with insolence. Then, he noticed that a legion of rats, the biggest and the longest he had ever seen, came in and out of the cracks between the bags. [...] Well-fed rats! He shivered in thinking of what food they were feeding off". (*Death of a Hero* – Richard Aldington).

"The dead had their faces in the mud, or they emerged from dugouts, peaceful, hands resting on the edge, head lying on their arms. The rats came to sniff them, jumped from one dead to another. They chose the young first, without a beard on their cheeks. They sniffed the cheek then curled up and started to eat the flesh from the nose to the mouth, then the edge of the lips and the cheek. From time to time they passed their paw in their whiskers to get clean. For the eyes, they took them out with little claws, and licked the eyeball hole, then, biting into the eye like in a small egg, they chewed gently, mouth sideways smelling the juice". (*Le Grand Troupeau* – Jean Giono).

As for the lice, man's relentlessness to eradicate rats has no noticeable effect. Ratters, cats, poison, stalking only provoke derisory losses in the ranks of the opponent. In 1916, there was even the idea of proposing to men a bonus for every rat killed, To validate their hunt and collect the amount due, it was up to them to submit to the officer the tails of vanquished rats. " A cook who had read the decision announced that now he would be allocated a bonus of one penny (five cents) for each destroyed rat. All he had to do to get paid was to present the tails to the sergeant-major. [...] So ring finders, Boche button crimpers, initial chiselers, hammers of copper and aluminum smelters – all handymen trench art, turned their ingenuity towards this lucrative hunt". (*Mémoires d'un rat* – Pierre Chaine).

✦ German dog posing in front of his catch, Pontivart, 1915. Historial de la Grande Guerre, Péronne.

Administration Communale de Gosselies

CHATS

L'Autorité allemande nous prie d'informer le public de son désir d'acheter les chats.

Les propriétaires qui voudraient vendre leurs chats, peuvent s'adresser à la Gendarmerie où il leur sera payé de 5 à 4 Mk. par bête.

Gosselies, le 11 Mai 1918.

Le ff. Bourgmestre,
Em. MOUSTY.

impr. L. PIRON, Gosselies.

✦ German poster for the populations of the occupied zones, Gosselies, 11 May 1918. Historial de la Grande Guerre, Péronne.

✦ Poster: "Sell your rabbit skins to traders and breeders, the army needs them", Germany, 1917. Historial de la Grande Guerre, Péronne.

1914
1915
1916
1917
1918

Reading this poster challenges: why the hell do the Germans want to buy cats? No sources, no known testimonials to this day bring any answers. It is therefore necessary to make assumptions.

- In the face of severe dietary restrictions in Germany, was there any thought in 1918 of proposing cat meat on the menu of the soldiers? It seems unlikely, even if the testimony of Blaise Cendrars, already presented, attests that some cats finished at the bottom of the pot (see page 16).

- The soldiers suffered from the cold during the hard winters of war. Have we considered providing them with warm protection made of cat fur (mittens, boots...) to protect them from diseases and frostbite? A German poster seems to show through the example of the rabbit that this hypothesis remains plausible.

- The most likely hypothesis is that we expected in cats what men had failed to accomplish: eradicate rats in the trenches but also in the storage at the rear, where commodities, textiles, leather... were stocked. An article in the Cingoli Gazette, a French trench newspaper of the 107th heavy artillery-regiment, dated December 1917, shows the helplessness of men against this scourge and the hope to see the cats help them: "We're asking for cats because the rats are getting involved in the group's Personnel conditions, there are too many rodents that have eaten the prepared permissions. Thanks to the speed of links, these have been redone without delay for the lucky beneficiaries. But what emotion! Cats, please".

THE SYMBOLS

NATIONAL EMBLEMS AND PROPAGANDA

In popular imagery, animals have always translated with force some positive traits (the fidelity of the dog) or negative ones (the perfidy of the snake). Eagle, rooster, lion and others embody as well the nations engaged in the First World War, a total war where the mobilisation of spirits pushed the patriotism to its climax.

Through thoughtful propaganda, every belligerent largely used these personified symbols to rally the determination of the nation, the resistance fiercely opposed to the enemy and, of course, to announce the inevitable victory. These symbolic animals provided an effective lever to elaborate strong messages, simple to interpret and without equivocal.

We see it through the posters below on the right, a transfer takes place. A cock crushing the enemy or a French "Poilu" strangling the German eagle. We no longer just fight man against man but man against man's animal emblem. The latter does not represent no longer just "an" enemy but the enemy nation as a whole.

✦ British recruitment poster, the young lions refer to British dominions and colonies. Historial de la Grande Guerre, Péronne.

✦ German ceremonial helmet, surmounted with the imperial eagle. Historial de la Grande Guerre, Péronne.

✦ Poster for the first French war loan, Abel Faivre, 1915. Historial de la Grande Guerre, Péronne.

✦ Poster for the fourth and last French war loan, Marcel Falter, 1918. Historial de la Grande Guerre, Péronne.

✦ Patriotic plate, "Verdun 1916, Will not pass! We will have them!" Mr. Zillhardt. *Historial de la Grande Guerre, Péronne.*

✦ Statuette. French cock dominating the enemy, symbolised by the pointed helmet and a snake hiding underneath. *Historial de la Grande Guerre, Péronne.*

On other illustrations, the man simply disappears in favour of these symbols alone.

It's a real bestiary that the propaganda staged to achieve its goals. In a conflict where everyone esteems himself in his right, where everyone claimed to lead a defensive war against threat or aggressive enemy, it was about proving that the war we were waging was just.

DOGS OF WAR

✦ Map of Europe, "Hark! Hark! the dogs do bark!" , Great Britain, 1914. *Historial de la Grande Guerre, Péronne.*

The Triple Entente kept the central powers in check. All were represented by dogs, with the exception of Russia, represented by a "steam roller", due to its superior demographic reserve. Note that it was a dachshund, which embodies Germany, a dog seemingly harmless – at first. This funny choice was ultimately logical since the German Kaiser Wihelm II was surrounded all his life by these pet dogs.

Le Petit Journal

SUPPLEMENT ILLUSTRE

DIMANCHE 20 SEPTEMBRE 1914

SUS AU MONSTRE !

✦ *Le Petit Journal*, "Sus au monstre!", La France, 20 September 1914. The "monstre" - monster, as indicates the headgear on the dragon's head, is no other than the alliance of the central powers: Germany and Hungro-Austria. Source: Gallica.bnf.fr.

7. Kriegsanleihe

WILSON

Ein Deutscher wäre tief gesunken, gäb' er dem Wilson, dem Halunken, der drüben freche Reden führt, die Antwort nicht, die ihm gebührt. Drum Brüder, gebt mit offner Hand dem Land der alten Barden, dem freien, deutschen Vaterland, zum Schwertschliff die Milliarden!

FRITZ BALDAUF (Bd.III)

✦ Poster for the 7th German War Loan presenting the US President Wilson as a dragon, Fritz Baldauf, 1917. Historial de la Grande Guerre, Péronne.

DESTROY THIS MAD BRUTE

ENLIST

It was the war of civilisation against barbarism or, in a more Manichean way, good against evil. In that context, it was accepted to make the enemy a monster. By choosing animals that inspired mistrust, fear, disgust, it dehumanised them in everyone's eyes, and especially those of the neutral countries of which one wished to attract their favours. In such a procedure, it's no wonder a mirror effect was observed, each camp used, in the end, the same strategy to tarnish the image of the other, even if German propaganda remained less virulent in that area.

Conversely, animating the enemy can also lead to laughter. And propaganda does not stop there! By ridiculing the enemy, making him a subject of mockery, it reached the goal just as effectively: to harm the image, the reputation of the other. Of course, there were other animals that took over: pig, plucked eagle or chicken, fleeing rabbit...

✦ Poster calling for volunteers, "Destroy this mad brute", United States, Harry Rile Hopps, 1917. Australian War Memorial, Canberra.

✦ French porcelain Mustard pot. The helmet allows us to immediately identify the enemy, is the mustard lid. Its tip provides a secure hold for lifting. Historial de la Grande Guerre, Péronne.

THE MASCOTS

The *"Petit Larousse 2017"* gives the mascot the following definition: "Person or animal considered lucky, fetish". Here, only animal mascots will be presented, without going back to simple pet animals mentioned earlier and who brought fighters affection and comfort (see page 14). Mascots are animals adopted by an extended group of men (a regiment or a battalion, for example), which allowed to differentiate them from pet animals, attached to an individual or a small core of men.

✦ Kangaroo mascot of the 9th and 10th Australian Infantry battalions, Egypt, December 1914. Australian War Memorial, Canberra.

In some regiments, the choice of the mascot was related to the very origins of the soldiers. What better to maintain the morale of the troops than an animal representative of the fauna of the native country: a kangaroo, a wallaby or a koala among the Australians, a springbok among South Africans…

Others were the result of unexpected encounters thanks to the movements of the troops: brought together when animals approached in search of food, injured animals taken in and cared for or stray animals caught. In these cases, in addition to cats and dogs, were amazing mascots who learnt to tolerate and accept cohabitation with man, to be tamed and sometimes to learn from them. Like those talking birds who acquired in contact with soldiers a military vocabulary: "Fire!", "Alert!", "Boche"… Objects of much attention – even when the food was lacking, men do not hesitate to sacrifice a share of their meagre pittance – without doubt they also end up finding an interest in them. It was an exchange of good practices, of a relationship where everyone gave and received.

IN THE STREETS OF PERONNE

When on September 1, 1918, the Australians finally freed Péronne and were installed there, they renamed several streets with names referring to their distant country (Wombat Road, Wallaby Lane ...). A strange street sign was erected on the facade of City Hall for the 80th anniversary of the liberation of the town; a reminder of their passage: the "Kanga Roo"! A name enigmatic but that makes sense when mixing the French and English languages. What should have been named according to English grammar "Kanga Roo" ("Rue" – French for street becoming with the English pronunciation roo) becomes in Frenchifying the formulation "Kanga Roo", the "Kangaroo Street".

RooDeKanga   **WombatRd**

✦ Wooden street signs, 1918.
Australian War Memorial, Canberra.

Roo de Kanga
1918-1998
We do not Forget Australia

✦ Existing street sign on the Town hall of Péronne.

✦ Guigui boar mascot of a French gunners section, Hesse forest, 23 July 1915. BDIC, Fonds Valois.

✦ The Budah monkey, mascot of a Belgian lancers squadron, Houthem, 18 August 1916. BDIC, Fonds Valois.

"Cigognes", storks. We naturally find many birds (eagle, swallow, rooster...) but also a multitude of other animals (rabbit, wolf, panther...) less accustomed to altitude but possessing, for the most part, qualities searched for by the pilots during the aerial duels. The mascot revealed himself in turn as, agile, obstinate, elusive, predatory... The whole thing was ultimately a formidable bestiary.

✦ Georges Guynemer posing in front of his plane "Le Vieux Charles" - Old Charles, Le Hamel, 1916. BDIC, Fonds Valois.

The definition of the *Petit Larousse* can however, be extended beyond just people and animals and their representations. These representations almost exclusively animal are found again and again in the regimental insignia and federate each group around a true symbolic referent. The example of the British infantry regiments is probably the most evocative.

✦ Prancing Horse, Royal West Kent Regiment. Historial de la Grande Guerre, Péronne. ✦ Eagle of King's Regiment (Liverpool). Historial de la Grande Guerre, Péronne.

This category of mascots was very present in aviation. Pilots left free rein to their imagination and proudly adorned their fetish animal on the flanks of their machines (over 50% of their mascots were from the animal world). The most famous example is undoubtedly the one of Georges Guynemer's squadron, known as the

✦ Antilope of the 1st Pals' Battalion, Birmingham. Historial de la Grande Guerre, Péronne.

FROM PICASSO TO CHAMELEON

In a war where to hide in the eyes of the enemy was a necessity, the French army innovates and, on the initiative of Lucien-Victor Guirand of Scévola and Louis Guingot, created the first camouflage* unit in February 1915. Inspired by artistic movements such as Cubism and fauvism, the section worked so that men, materials and infrastructure (railways, airfields, etc.) melted into the environment. When Guirand of Scévola wondered about their future mascot, the choice was obviously the Chameleon, champion of all categories in camouflage, as he applies to drawing on himself.

✦ Armband for the camouflage units. Historial de la Grande Guerre, Péronne.

"I remember being with Picasso in Boulevard Raspail at the beginning of the war, that we saw the first camouflaged guns pass us by. It was evening, we had heard about camouflage, but we had not seen them yet and Picasso, marveling, was looking, then exclaimed: Yes, it's us that did that, us! It's Cubism!" (Gertrude Stein, Picasso, 1938).

* From the Italian *camuffare*: camouflage, disguise, hide.

THE GRATITUDE

THE HEROES OF WAR

Many soldiers were decorated for their sacrifice and their feats of arms. During or after the war, citations and medal honours were awarded to them, sometimes posthumous title. Although sharing with the fighters the miseries and the suffering, and even though proportionally their rate of losses were even higher, only one hundred and twenty thousand animals were given a citation or were decorated – mainly among the Germans and the British, the French were less charitable. Among these elected officials, dogs and pigeons became true "heroes of war". However, no horse left his name in the pantheon of animals; but about ten thousand German horses were awarded post-war medals for "Services made" by a Bavarian association.

✦ German enamel medal bearing the Iron Cross for the horses "comrades of war". Memorial of Verdun.

"Saved his unit by signaling the presence of a large unsuspected column of German soldiers. By his barking, he aroused the attention of his driver who, having gone forward, recognised the presence of the enemy and tied a message to the dog's collar, who returned to the French lines and the alert was given". This quotation showcases the Pyrame, a sentinel auxiliary in a battalion of French alpine hunters. He was awarded a star, a scout insignia, by the president Raymond Poincaré in person who took notice of his actions during his visit to the front of Alsace in 1917.

Like the Pyrame, other canine auxiliaries were recognised by the order of the French army for reporting the approach of enemy patrols and permitting them to push them back or sometimes even to capture them: Lion (registration number 147), Fox (registration number 221), Diane (registration number 234)...

Stubby, serving in an American infantry regiment, remains after his many exploits the most decorated dog of the Great War. Smuggled into France by his master, he participated in four great offensives and seventeen battles during which he was particularly effective: he alerted the soldiers of the arrival of the gases, located wounded in no man's land, transmitted messages, warned of the arrival of enemy patrols... Promoted Sergeant, he became the first "senior" dog of the US Army and at the same time, superior to his Master, Robert Coroy, simple Corporal! His exploits had such a

resonance in the United States that on his death in 1927, he was mounted and exhibited ever since in the Smithsonian Museum in Washington.

Like their four-legged friends, pigeons such as Vaillant and Cher Ami have demonstrated heroism. Vaillant stood out during the battle of Verdun in 1916. While the commander Sylvain Raynal and his men defended the fort from Vaux. Surrounded by the Germans, the siege of the

✦ Sergeant Stubby with his medals.

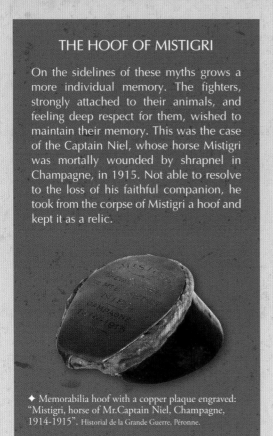

THE HOOF OF MISTIGRI

On the sidelines of these myths grows a more individual memory. The fighters, strongly attached to their animals, and feeling deep respect for them, wished to maintain their memory. This was the case of the Captain Niel, whose horse Mistigri was mortally wounded by shrapnel in Champagne, in 1915. Not able to resolve to the loss of his faithful companion, he took from the corpse of Mistigri a hoof and kept it as a relic.

✦ Memorabilia hoof with a copper plaque engraved: "Mistigri, horse of Mr.Captain Niel, Champagne, 1914-1915". Historial de la Grande Guerre, Péronne.

fight, although the action takes place during the Second World War. Like Stubby, the serial hero 787-15 was mounted and is kept in the museum of the Military Colombophile of Mount Valerian.

Cher Ami (Dear friend in French), was a pigeon serving in the American army, that delivered at least twelve messages during his time of service. But it was in the forest of Argonne, in July 1918, that he realised his most famous mission. While a battalion found himself isolated, cut off from his lines, and several couriers had already paid with their lives in their attempts to reconnect with the closest units, Cher Ami tried his luck. Under violent German fire, he reached the neighbouring general headquarters and delivered his message. Informed of the situation, the command successfully sent reinforcements to clear the encircled battalion. Losing a foot, taken by shrapnel as well as a lot of blood, Cher Ami was greatly weakened but recovered. General Pershing awarded him the American War Cross for services rendered to the nation, and was repatriated to the United States.

fortress lasted for a hundred days, fighting with the grenades and machine guns the defenders were exhausted. On June 4, ammunition, food and water were lacking. Vaillant, their last pigeon, was their last resort to report to headquarters that the position had become unbearable. In the middle of the gas and fumes, he took off. Heavily intoxicated by the gas, he managed, never-the-less to return to the military dovecote of Verdun and deliver the precious message. Unfortunately the attempts to defend failed and the Commander Raynal was forced to surrender on June 7. In recognition of his bravery, Vaillant was cited to the order of the French army and was awarded a ring of honour: "Despite the enormous difficulties resulting from intense smoke and abundant gas, he accomplished the mission which had been entrusted to him by Major Raynal. A unique means of communication by the heroic defender of Fort Vaux, brought the last information to be received from this heavily intoxicated officer, who arrived dying at the dovecote". The legend of the pigeon of Fort de Vaux passed on for posterity and inspired in 2005, an animated feature film: Vaillant, pigeon of

✦ Statuette representing the pigeon named Vaillant, "Souvenir of Verdun, the last pigeon of Fort de Vaux", Richer. Historial de la Grande Guerre, Péronne.

✦ Postcard of the plaque commemorating the feat of the homing pigeon that carried the last message.
Historial de la Grande Guerre, Péronne.

COMMEMORATIVE PLAQUES, MONUMENTS AND MEMORIALS

Monuments and memorials dedicated to fighters are innumerable: monuments to the dead of our villages, regimental steles, national memorials... But, although some sites commemorate their massive participation in the conflict, animals appear as forgotten history. Forgotten at least in past time because since the eighties, interest in these fellow soldiers sees a renewed interest. This manifests itself in particular by inaugurating new memorial sites; this phenomenon is confirmed by the exhibitions and recent books dealing with animals during the Great War.

These sites pay tribute to the main animals that were mobilised and direct actors during the war. We thus find dogs, pigeons, horses, sometimes donkeys and mules. It is however noted that depending on the sites, the animal appears alone or alongside men they have rubbed shoulders with. Without being exhaustive, the table here is a selection:

		Mobilized Animals represented	
		Alone	In the company of a personage
Commemorative plaques		**Pigeons:** Fort de Vaux (France), Brussels, Belgium), Charleroi (Belgium) **Horses:** Saumur (France) **Horses and mules:** Washington (United States) **Mules:** Neuville-lès-Vaucouleurs (France)	
Monuments		**Horses:** Nantillois (France) **Pigeons:** Charleroi (Belgium)	**Dogs:** Pagny-sur-Moselle (France) Saint-Menehould (France) Brussels, (Belgium) **Horses:** Chipilly (France) Paris (France) Minneapolis (United States) **Pigeons:** Lille (France) Binarville (France) Brussels (Belgium) **Mules /Donkeys:** Arras (France) Canberra (Australia)
Memorials		**All:** Couin (France) Pozières (France) London (Great Britain)	

✦ Monument to homing pigeons in Lille, France: erected in 1936 by the "fédération nationale des sociétés colombophiles", the monument is dedicated "To the 20,000 pigeons that died for the homeland" and "to pigeon fanciers shot by the enemy for detaining homing pigeons". A swarm of homing pigeons in flight revolve around an allegory of peace. One of them crushes a snake, symbol of the vanquished enemy.
Rémi Vouters collection.

✦ War Monument in Pagny-sur-Moselle, France: alert and fully trained, the dog sentinel stands equal to the French Poilu that accompanies him, the heroic defender of the sacred soil of the homeland. Jean-François Genet collection.

✦ Chipilly Monument, France, is dedicated to the 58th British Division: a gunner craddles a wounded horse. On the monument is the inscription "*Pro deo, pro rece, pro patria*" (" For God, for the King, for the Fatherland").
Yazid Medmoun collection.

1914

1915

1916

1917

The Australian Animal War Memorial in Pozières (France), a village where Australians delivered a furious battle in 1916, pays homage to the fallen Australian animals during the war but more widely to animals of all kinds and of all nations. Made up of different sections, the site was inaugurated on July 21, 2017 and shows the interest aroused today by the tragic fate of these animals.

✦ The memorial in Pozières, France, is dedicated to officers and soldiers of the Australian Army Veterinary Corps (AAVC). "They brought comfort and care to war animals".

✦ "We honour and thank them. Despite the horror of the battle, they gave their all. [...] This choice was not not theirs, but their courage has been great [...]".

✦ "To all animals. They helped without malice. They served all the countries. They worked and died at the service of men".

SIMPSON AND HIS DONKEY

Created in 1965, the Simpson medal commemorates the 50th anniversary of Battle of Gallipoli, in the Dardanelles Strait. It was given to all veterans and the families of the missing. It refers directly to Private John Simpson Kirkpatrick, a paramedic whose name became synonymous with bravery and compassion in Australia. During the battle, Simpson and his donkey, inseparable heroes in Australian remembrance, recovered many wounded on the field of battle and brought them back to the first aid stations. After four weeks of intense activity, Simpson was fatally wounded and since has embodied, to the highest degree, the spirit of sacrifice demonstrated by Australians during the Great War. A monument is dedicated to this famous pair in Canberra. Their story also inspired a children's literature book called Simpson and his donkey (Mark Greenwood and Frané Lessac, 2008).

✦ Simpson medal, ANZAC 1915.
Franco-Australian Museum, Villers-Bretonneux.

✦ Simpson and his donkey carrying a wounded soldier, Gallipoli, 1915.
Australian War Memorial, Canberra

Alongside these animal actors in the conflict, many totem animals have imposed themselves on sites and memorials: the caribou in Beaumont-Hamel (France), Masnières (France), Gueudecourt (France), Monchy-le-Preux (France); the eagle at Château-Thierry (France), Pontfaverger (France), Thiaucourt (France), Illfurth (France); the dragon at Mametz (France); the stork in Poelkapelle (Belgium); Lion in Chaulnes (France), Beaumont-Hamel (France), Souville (France), Varvinay (France), Braye-en-Laonnois (France), Munster (France), Nieuwpoort (Belgium), Ploegsteert (Belgium) ; the pelican at Havrincourt (France); the bulldog Belleau wood (France)...

These animals were chosen because of their strong symbolic power. They represent a nation, a philosophy. Here, is no longer evoked the suffering endured by their congeners but the sacrifice of men.

1914

1915

1916

1917

1918

✦ Pelican monument Havrincourt , France, dedicated to the 62nd West Riding Division.

✦ Newfoundland Caribou dominates the field of Battle of Beaumont-Hamel, France. The animal is installed on a rocky promontory, at the highest point of the site. He stands up strongly against the German positions of summer 1916.
Laurent Mariaud collection

✦ Dragon monument in Mametz, France, dedicated to the 38th Welsh Division. The animal holds in its claws strands of barbed wire, symbols of the enemy trenches he faces.

31

CONCLUSION

The wars of the late 19th century announced a major turning point, largely related to modernisation of the armament. The armies of 1914 had to achieve structural feats, strategic and economic new methods of combat. Now, material means were gaining in importance over the belligerents ability to recruit ever larger numbers of men.

If in 1914 "the artillery prepares and the infantry conquers", after the battles of Verdun and the Somme in 1916, "the cannon conquers and the infantry occupies". Historiography has, from very early on, been interested in the consequences that the industrialisation of the battlefield had on the soldiers: miserable living conditions, brutalisation of combatants, mass death... But it has long omitted to associate with the martyrdom of men that of the enlisted animals. Animal soldiers who, quoting the inscription on the monument dedicated to them in London in 2004, "They had no choice".

Fourteen million enlisted and ten million killed! Horses, dogs and others suffered just as much as the infantry and artillerymen. Although many testimonials and photographs attest their presence, their suffering and their indispensable role in the conduct of war, had to wait until the beginning of the eighties before we see historians, and the general public in general, begin to care and be moved by the animals condition during the Great War.

It must be remembered that, despite the mechanisation, no army would have been able to lead and to continue the war without their help. It was not possible to get rid of their valuable participation and animals, like men, adapted to the evolution of the battlefield: the dog for example, in the beginning a first aid assistant, became a sentry then a messenger in the last part of the conflict. This dedicated and selfless collaboration remained effective, to a lesser extent perhaps, during the Second World War. The penny flipped in the second half of the 20th century when vehicles, more and more efficient, and the incessant technological innovations are an undivided domination, finally offered animals "a well deserved retirement".

Today, only dogs, the horse no longer used for anything other than during parades, retain a place in theatres of war. Their missions have evolved and are no longer necessarily for those led by their counterparts of the Great War. Advanced training intended for the research and detection of explosives, search of weapons or narcotics, for protection or to be used as scouts. In France, the quota amounts to four hundred and fifty dogs in the Army, twelve RAID and four in the GIGN (we must add the dogs of the national police assigned to surveillance and control missions against crime on the public streets). Fewer, but just as indispensable as in the past, they are recognised as full military and are rewarded on a par with their human counterparts (the highest distinction being the Gold Medal of the National Defense). Even though they are pampered and their living conditions can not be compared to those known by the dogs of the trenches, the risk is still part of their daily life. Sacrifice too! Diesel, a 7-year-old Malinois Belgian shepherd, was killed in an assault launched on November 18, 2015 against the terrorists who had sowed chaos in Saint-Denis, Paris five days earlier.

✦ Departure of the first aid ambulance dogs for the Front Line, 1915.
Historial de la Grande Guerre, Péronne.